# GOD AND THE TREE AND ME

## Dorothy Hanson Brown

*Illustrated by Susan Fiorenzo*

The Upper Room

The quotation from Meister Eckhart on page 4 is taken from page 32 in MEISTER ECKHART: A MODERN TRANSLATION, translated by Raymond B. Blakney. Copyright 1941 by Harper & Row, Publishers, Inc. Used by permission of the Publisher.

The excerpt on page 11 is from a review by Frederick Buechner, "Summons to Pilgrimage," which first appeared in *The New York Times,* March 16, 1969, © 1969 by The New York Times Company. Reprinted by permission.

Excerpts from the poems "Remembering" and "Initial" by Rainer Maria Rilke are reprinted from TRANSLATIONS FROM THE POETRY OF RAINER MARIA RILKE by M. D. Herter Norton, with the permission of W. W. Norton & Company, Inc. Copyright 1938 by W. W. Norton & Company, Inc. Copyright renewed 1966 by M. D. Herter Norton.

The quotation appearing on page 55 is reprinted by permission of Schocken Books, Inc. from TEN RUNGS: HASIDIC SAYINGS, edited by Martin Buber. Copyright © 1947 by Schocken Books, Inc. Copyright renewed © 1975 by Schocken Books, Inc.

The excerpt from the poem "His Answer" by Martin Buxbaum appearing on page 73 is taken from WHISPERS IN THE WIND by Martin Buxbaum published by World Publishing and © 1966 by Martin Buxbaum. Used by permission of Harry N. Abrams.

First Printing, July, 1979 (8)
Library of Congress Catalog Card Number: 79-66196
ISBN: 0-8358-0386-4
Printed in the United States of America

*To Hal*
*who is making all*
*things new*

For God does not give gifts, nor did he ever
give one, so that man might keep it and take
satisfaction in it; but all were given—all he
ever gave on earth or in heaven—that he
might give this one more: himself. . . .
Therefore I say that we must learn to look
through every gift and every event to
God. . . . There is no stopping place in this
life—no, nor was there ever one for any man,
no matter how far along his way he'd gone.
This above all, then, be ready at all times for
the gifts of God and always for new ones.

MEISTER ECKHART

# Contents

# Preface

This book is a savoring of life in the confidence that God is in the midst of all of it; that he reveals himself, not only in the areas of our lives about which we talk in reverent tones, but also in the pain, frustration, regret, and joyfulness of our everyday lives. Truth, when it is come upon by surprise, is found in small packages, as when one turns a corner in a well-used path, and finds a treasure in the high grass. Finally, it is a celebration of the worthiness of all people, whether they be lovely or unlovely, simply because they are God's creation, and loved by him. Robert Béla Wilhelm sums it well:

> Rather than impose a theology—or a spirituality—on our lives from the outside, we need to be sensitive to the ways in which God becomes known to us in our daily experience. Somehow, we need to be able to identify, record, evaluate, and nurture our experience of the sacred within the core of our being. Like Tolstoy, we must accept the full impact of Jesus' statement that "The kingdom of God is within you." That is, God is present in our experiences; and salvation history must be found in the story of our own inner lives.

Experiential theology expresses itself through our
personal mythologies. The persons, the events,
the dreams, the memories, and all the elements of
our experience come together in a unique story
that only we can tell. Our story is irreplaceable, a
unique flowering of God's presence in human life.
The importance of each life story is summarized
by Nikos Kazantzakis through the character of
Zorba the Greek: Zorba knows that the
uniqueness of his life is a beautiful and fragile
thing, and that his story cannot be separated from
his life. Zorba says, "When I die, the whole
zorbatic world dies with me."[1]

I had never thought of it in quite that way. But
I remember standing at the bedside of my mother. I
had not been out of her hospital room for half an
hour, when she died, unexpectedly. I remember
returning, numb and resentful. She was too young
to die. Her skin was unwrinkled. There was scarcely
a strand of gray in her hair. But more than
resentment, there was emptiness, for she was gone,
and suddenly I realized that I didn't know her. We
had lived together all these years, but not once that
I could remember had she let me come inside to see
the person she really was or to know her dreams.
She was gone, and I and the child within me had
lost, irreplaceably.
So when Wilhelm asks, "How, then, can I
celebrate my own unique story—the epiphany of

[1]"The Progoff Journal Process," *Liturgy: Journal of the Liturgical
Conference,* May 1976, vol. 21, no. 5.

God's presence in the world through my life?"[2] I can
answer, "With this giving of myself." I can reveal
something of myself, so that some may say, "I feel
that I know her. She asks these questions of life;
she dreams these dreams." And knowing, they may
understand more of themselves.

It is said that Michelangelo once struggled to
push a huge piece of rock down the street. An
onlooker asked him why he labored over so old a
piece of stone. Michelangelo replied, "Because there
is an angel in the rock that wants to come out."
There is something in my life that usurps my days
and keeps me awake at night. Something that wants
to come out.

I have a deep sense of gratitude for a beloved
high school English teacher who opened windows;
for those who have been *lenders of the mind* in
books; for special friends who listened and believed;
for my children who nodded sagely and hugged me
warmly when they read; for Susan Jones Fiorenzo
who caught the meanings with her artist's pen; and
for Lucile "Sissie" Vahldieck who patiently
transcribed my hieroglyphics.

Progoff says, "We all go down our private
wells, but the underlying stream at the bottom flows
through everyone's well."[3] I would wish it to be so
for you and me.

DOROTHY HANSON BROWN

[2]Ibid.
[3]Ibid.

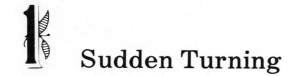

# Sudden Turning

We are all of us more mystics than we believe
or choose to believe. . . . We have seen more
than we let on, even to ourselves. Through
some moment of beauty or pain, some sudden
turning of our lives, we catch glimmers at
least of what the saints are blinded by, only
then, unlike the saints, we tend to go on as
though nothing has happened. To go on as
though someting *has* happened, even though
we are not sure what it was or just where we
are supposed to go with it, is to enter the
dimension of life that religion is a word for.

FREDERICK BUECHNER

# Parable

I found a tiny maple tree
among the dried-up spears
of last year's iris leaves
and marveled
that so small a thing
could have survived the winter.

*Tree*, itself, may be too large,
for it was just a seedling,
stem, two leaves,
and root.

It said to me,
"You wonder?

"Before this, I was seed with wings.
Kamikaze-like
I stabbed the earth,
not knowing that in time
its warm, dark womb
would nourish me.

"Before that, I was tree.
I put my arms out to the sun
and felt the wind and rain
and sheltered life."

My knees made hollows
in the soil.
I heard myself replying,
"So with me.
I shelter life
   that will give life
      that will give life
         that will give life.
God and the tree and me."

# North Country

The stream struggles with the rocks
and tugs at logs that strew its path;
so choked with windfalls,
tree on tree, it could not even
dream itself a river.

Strength conserved,
it tumbles down the slope
among the moss and lichen
and the polished roots of birch trees.
In the sand, where only ducks and geese
have left their mark,
it carves a winding ribbon to the shore
and melds its life with Lake Superior.

What law of nature gives command
for winding?
In the sand there is no hindrance,
rock or tree.

Late sun, walking on the water,
touches it with silver;
and the silver touches me.

Nature has a way with water,
pilgrim water returning to the sea.

God, why can't I yield
as easily as water?

# gray is a word for living

patient
the old barn leans
against the wind
and shuts its mind to
coldness
sifting through the rafters.
it thinks of pussy willows
bursting into velvet
and newborn rabbits
squeaking
in the nest.

gray
is a day beginning
before the sun
has pulled away the mist
and tinged the edges
lavender.
I touch the eyelids
of my newborn child;
her ears are pink as seashells
her baby fingers curled.

gray
is the tangle
of December woods
against a sulphur sky.
leaves scamper
over snow-crust.
my father's face is parchment
stretched on bone.
I stroke his fingers.

gray
is a word
for death.

# The Will of Things

Now cattails slake their thirst
in withered ponds
and Queen Anne's Lace
runs rampant in the dust.
Patchwork daisies
conquer rocky hillsides.

City women fan themselves
in doorways;
dusty poplars
fan a denim sky.
Querulous
the robin pecks
and calls for rain.

Once there was a city field
where daisies grew.
A spring-fed brook
kept houses at their distance.
I waded knee-deep
in the unmown grass
to pick white petals,
counting, "Love me, love me not";
or used my tongue
to split the milky stems
for making chains
and wore them in my hair.

Deep within this asphalt tomb
that steams and simmers
in the August sun,
brook and daisies are long gone.
Yet knowing something
of the will of things . . .
I wonder.

# Gently from the Night

Stars had scarcely given way.
The moon, reluctant to retire,
maintained its right to stay.
Ground fog born of cold night air
and warmer sand
drifted over shoreline.

Weary from a night
that brought no fish,
they trimmed their sail
and bent their backs
the hundred yards remaining,
when some hail-fellow
on the shore shouted,
"How's your catch?"

Expletives were smothered
in their beards
until they saw him cup his hands
and halloo,
"Shoot your nets to starboard!"
And now their muscles ached
with pulling in what nets
the boat would hold
and towing others.

Peter wading through the surf
was first to see
the charcoal fire
and smell the fish upon it
and hear the invitation,
"Breakfast is ready.
Come and eat!"

Their senses spun;
they needed time
to make some logic
of this man
whose eyes and voice
and stance
were
just the same.

No one dared
to ask his name,
but each man knew
within himself,
and gently from the night
there came the warmth of morning.

# Yearning

Sometimes in April
when the wind is chill
and daffodils do not yet dare
commit themselves to blooming,
    there is a shade of day,
    gray-lavender,
    when sun breaks through the layered clouds
    and blesses willow trees.

A transient moment
caught and held
like a bubble from a child's pipe.
    Trees are green without their leaves,
    houses are painted sunset.

I feel myself transported,
walking along a country road
with the other women,
    straining to hear a word from
    One whose presence
    is a shaft of light.

## Holy Ground

Photographed inside
the canopy of pine trees
it made a lacy silhouette
against September sky.

We had to look again
to see a bush
so eaten up with beetles
its leaves were filigree.
Veins and stems
could crumble at a touch.

We thought
how beautiful a pattern
despite the handicap.

So with life.
God doesn't wait
until we're perfect.

# All about Us, On Their knees

Sometimes I watch them.

The old ones coming to the altar
kneel with pain,
a helping hand beneath the elbow.
The buoyant young
kneel with grace,
their backs as straight as aspen.

The little man
with Old World tongue
who polishes the floors
sinks to his knees
beside the magnate
in his correct gray suit.

Each brings his burden.
Deep inside he hides
his loneliness
or emptiness
or fear
and kneeling
gropes for meaning;
is aware of fragmentary truth
that blows across his mind.

O touch the one beside you!
If one suffers
so do we;
if one lifts up his head
and smiles,
we can sing.

All about us, on their knees
the body of our Lord.

# Once, In Passing

Fresh snow has fallen,
snow on snow.
It fills the street.
I walk one lane.
My little trees are burdened to the ground.
They await permission from the sun
to rise again.

The purple plum has other blossoms now,
branches full against the lantern light.
The garden sleeps
in rounded shapes like rooms
sheet-shrouded for a while,
awaiting life to lift their drape.

O God, how vast your sky,
how deep your snow!

Yet one small flake
caught on my sleeve,
I wonder at its form.
It says your love is greater
than the storm, and present
here with me.

# Stableboy

*Suggested by Marc Chagall's*
*painting Peasant Village.*

He lives with dung,
but in his mind
he tends a Pegasus.

Dreams are made of sturdy stuff;
genie-like they rise above
the sweat of horses,
cabbage cooking,
and the sour-sweet smell
of babies.

And in some far and shining place
a stableboy can dance.

## The Poetry Reading

I listened to her voice
high-pitched, fragile
yet strangely strong
and calm.
Her thoughts were threads
spun from flax
upon a wheel.
They wove textures,
colors,
patterns.

Paths among the trees,
the way ahead emerging.
Sunlight filtered patterns
on the ground,
pools of sunlight.

Thought-threads,
thought-paths,
they led inside.

She opened the door so freely.

I could not speak.

The Awakening of Stones

And you wait, are awaiting the one thing
that will infinitely increase your life;
the powerful, the uncommon,
the awakening of stones,
depths turned towards you.
. . . . . . . . . . . . . . . . . . . . . . .
and you think of lands journeyed through,
of pictures, of the apparel
of women lost again.

RAINER MARIA RILKE
*from "Remembering"*

# Time Machine

Strange, things one remembers
    looking back, like
    chickens pecking near the porch
    or kicking in the barnyard dust
    after their heads were off;
    and horses, guzzling at the trough.
        Their harness jingles
        as they shake away the flies;
        their lips are leather.

Sunlight ventures partway in
    to hayracks, resting
    in the shadows field mice
    nibble long forgotten cornstalks.
        I am riding the shoulders
        of a tall young man
        up to the hayloft and down again.

The tenant house
    marked the bend of the road.
    I could venture that far
    towards town and back;
        The dust is soft between my toes.
        A grasshopper sits on Queen Anne's lace
        and plays his fiddle.

The twisted orchard
    on the hill rained apples
    meant for deer and cows,
    and some were good for people.
        I throw one to the lazy sow
        who pokes her snout against the pen
        and waits to find me foe or friend.

The privy
    out beyond the house
    had smooth warm seats
    built grown-up high.
    Knotholes spilled sunshine.
        I watch a spider spin its web;
        it walks on silk from door to floor.
        The catalogue has pictures.

Heat is the curtain
    at midday
    that screens the hills, the valley.
        A lady in a long blue dress
        is making pies, just child-size,
        and I am four.

# The Journey

Had she lived until October
she would have been one hundred and two,
one hundred and two and counting.

She left her body, one winter's day,
to meld her soul with God.
She of the cotton-candy hair piled high,
of the gnarled and gentle hands,
of the lace fichu collars and lavender cologne;
she of the great heart
and limitless love
left for an extended visit.

I remember the trip to Great-grandmother's house,
shoe-box lunches in hand.
I remember the rattling train
and the peanut vendor
who came through the car
and the water cooler down at the end.
And I sat there, short legs dangling,
dreaming the days ahead—
horses and pigs, and sweet-smelling hay
and high featherbeds.

She opened the door,
her faith in her hand, and
stepped out to a new adventure.

# Country Inn, Vermont

First frost of the season,
I know it's there before I look.
There is something in the quiet
as though the wind
in leaves still on the trees
is hushed
with a fingertip.

Frost-white mornings
were always good
for staying under covers;
for plunging pell-mell
down the stairs
to dress beside the stove.

The floor is cold beneath my feet.
Frost on rooftops,
frost on grass
is thickest where the barn and roof
make corners,
where the sun can't reach.
Chimney smoke disappears
in ozone.

It is not far
to where the child,
face against the frosted glass,
is breathing warmth
on fern and tree
to make a place for looking.

And I am almost there.

# Miniature

What is there about making beds
that is not wasted motion?
Dust settles down
the minute I have polished.
Food prepared with such great care
is gone within an hour.

But making beds is something else,
smoothing the sheets,
fluffing the pillows,
tucking in the edges—
    I am straightening the bedclothes
    of a restless child,
    tucking him in after prayers,
    smoothing the hair from his forehead.

A woman's fingers through the years
trace images that reappear.

# Over the River and through the Woods

*(for Chris)*

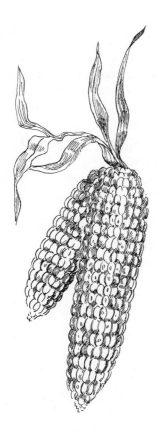

We hold to the paper husks of days
after the living is done.
We keep the molds of family days
and fill them again with remembering.
Food is a ritual;
the cooking conjures up the sights and sounds
and smells
of other days.

Nor will a new and shining way
suffice to feed the hunger in our hearts.

We reach to touch the lives
of those before
and those beyond;
they link us with the meaning
of all time.
New holidays will come,
new families will grow from ours,
and each will find the symbols
made to hold their love.

But just for now
we hold to us our rituals;
we live them once again.
They open up the secret places
of our hearts,
and we are thankful.

# Somewhere

There is another world of summer
made of sounds and tastes
and fragrances
that meld and mingle
like a dream:
the tinkle of the ice cream wagon bell
that sent us scurrying for nickles;
the coldness of a chunk of ice
melting on the tongue;
the night-borne smell
of honeysuckle.

Very near, hand-pushed mowers
echo down the street,
whirr and clatter.
I hear the screen doors banging;
children calling, "Ready or not, I'm coming—
all around the goal is it!"
at the corner street light;
children pleading for more time
from mothers herding them
to bed.

Sheets are cool on summer tan.
Wyeth-curtains catch a breeze
and float out over shingles.
Pictures float . . .
tomorrow's plans will wait
will . . . wait
until
tomorrow.

Downstairs
in the kitchen
grown-ups laugh and talk
and drink their coffee.

# Magnet

They say a full moon pulls the sea
and causes it to rise
flood tide.
This much I know:
it pulls at me.

Whiteness pours on floor
and chair and blanket.
An alabaster man beside me
stirs and mumbles in his sleep,
disturbed by dreams.

I cannot sleep.

Once, when I was ten
or thereabouts,
moonlight on my pillow wakened me.
I could have walked a path
from window
over rooftops
diamond-sprinkled
stretching house to house
to somewhere.
Moonlight was warm
and I was free as air.
It did not matter
I was bare beneath my nightdress.

This moon has shifted south to west
and looks in at another place;
so fast the earth has turned.
Embryonic poems churn my head
like waves that crest and break
and die in foam upon a shore.

The clock says four.

Throughway traffic starts again;
truckers hauling food and steel
for cities.
A vanquished silver dollar
sails the sky
letting go the houses
held within its spell.

And now they sleep.

## Reduction: To Change the Form but Not the Value

Sunlight through white curtains
is a master of reduction,
saying
this much is the essence,
this economy of setting will suffice;

this chair of moss green velvet,
creaking wood and faded velvet,
these reading glasses
folded
to mark a book of poems.

Bits of dust rise from the carpet,
from the roses in the carpet,
suspended
in the spotlight, like unfinished thoughts
disturbed.

For a moment
there's the feeling of another woman
rocking
and I, returning,
have a sense of having lived
before.

# The Storyteller

*After Joshua 4*


And the children asked,
"What are these stones
as we pass by . . .
these stones set up
like markers on the path?
What is their story?
What do they say?
Or did some traveler
in days gone by
stop here for rest
and idly occupy his hands,
his mind far down the road?"

And their leader said,
"This is the way
that we have come.
These stones mark
people, times,
and suffering.
They speak of dreams
and God."

# Dancing Tears

Out of infinite yearnings rise
finite deeds like feeble fountains,
that early and trembling droop.
But those, else silent within us,
our happy strengths—reveal themselves
in these dancing tears.

RAINER MARIA RILKE
*from "Initial"*

# Crusts

No one will remember
if I don't.
I was his birthday child.

He made it hard to love him.

Sometimes I'd lie awake and pray
that he'd come home.
I thought that if I prayed it
hard enough
I'd hear the bell
and Mama padding down the stairs.

Christmas mornings
when my skinny, dark ribbed stocking
bulged with orange
and chocolate
I knew that God had listened
or was it Santa Claus?

And even when his bed was empty
I could hope.

But I remember times
he'd hunt for berries,
come home stained and scratched;
he'd roll out dough and make an elderberry pie.

We were alone, together
when he died.

Salt-tears cannot soften
the crusts of words,
dry within the throat.

*O Papa, close your eyes and sleep.*
*Why can't I say*
*I love you?*

# Visiting Hours I

Her eyes are closed;
her head hangs down.
I rearrange her bandaged legs
and try to ease her pain.

Her husband sits beside the chair
and chirps a sailor's ditty. He says
he still remembers all the words,
and would we care to listen.

She does not hear
or if she does, she'd rather sleep.
The same flat tune through months and years
is worn into her brain.

I cannot reach her
any more than he.
My hand upon her arm
is touching flesh
and nothing more.

She cannot say a word
but something does.
We go, alone.

## II

Sunlight through the window
makes a halo of her hair
and warms her shoulders.
A puff of wind
could snuff her
like a dandelion.

She stretches blue-veined fingers
to the young man at her feet.
Bending forward until
their faces almost meet
she feels his hair
his cheeks
his beard.

Fingers are remembering.

Silently his eyes search hers
for symptom of their need;
gently, he draws her up
and tucks her hand
beneath his arm
and so they go to dinner.

She, somebody's mother,
he, somebody's son.

I think of Jesus
in a starched white coat
and pants.

# Reasonable Facsimile

Once, when the small life
she had sheltered seven months
was taken from her,
she fondled a white, porcelain lamb
someone had brought,
and was comforted.

Until the babies cried
across the hall.

# Recluse

They are taking out her life
in trash cans,
pieces of her life in plastic,
dumping them beside the street
to wait for garbage day.

Her children have not seen her
in the years
we have been neighbors,
but now they carry out
a box of something,
holding it away from clothes.

House for Sale and people hurry
prying, pushing, looking,
"There's a view from out this window,
a garden with some roses
and a tree."

Only those who stop and listen
hear a muffled cry, escaping;
see a small gray figure weeping
on the stairs.

# Requiem

Born a child of too few months,
they wrapped her well
in cotton
and warmed her
at the oven of the wood stove.

"Not strong enough to cope,"
they said
and never taught her better.

She died
a woman of few years
or so it seemed.
Her skin was soft.
I touched the thick, brown
braid upon the pillow
and smoothed the white cocoon of covers
on her bed.

Do you know I found your scrapbook
with the poems copied in it
and the violets pressed between the leaves,
and the crocheted lace
for handkerchiefs?

There was a picture of a house
that never was
with a picket fence
around it.

I never knew my mother
'til she died.

## On Coming Home from the Memorial Service

Lonely is not word enough
for one who feels death
coming,
but must wait awhile.

Eyes implore an affirmation:
"Look, I'm Fred.
I've lived, I'm living.
Watch with me."

"The day is fine,
the air is cool.
The children will be coming
home from school.
You're looking better every day."

Afraid to offer honest words
or tears
or touch,
we do not want to understand
too much
our own Gethsemane.

# Come Sing with Me

When a man is singing and
cannot lift his voice, and
another comes and sings with
him, another who can lift
his voice, the first will be able
to lift his voice too. That is
the secret of the bond between
spirits.

MARTIN BUBER

# Reflection

Here, at the bend of the stream,
the leaves float quietly,
caught in a pool the rocks have made.

The day is porcelain.
If I call to you, fresh leaves will fall.

I will sit here on this rock
and see if my frail, circling bark
will clear the dam
and dare the world.

# I Have Eaten Loveliness

The wind is playing games today.
It tickles the trees
with its fingers
until they, convulsed in laughter,
let go a rain of leaves
across the road.

Sunlight changes birches
into schoolgirls
running with the wind,
bending, turning,
gold hair flying,
"Come and catch me if you can!"

Fir trees, silent,
straight as soldiers,
dignified and darkly green,
lift their shaggy arms in protest;
scold the wind
and send the sun
to stand behind a cloud.

I have eaten loveliness like candy.
My eyes are weary.
I can taste no more.

## Summer's End, Magnolia

Now while prudent humans sleep
the moonlight beckons;
using leaves for patterns
it dapples lawns in liquid shapes
that glide, recede
and mingle.

There at the deepest shadow's edge
a rabbit stiffens.
Ears erect, he knows my presence,
ponders danger
and deeming me no more than statue
drops to nibble dew.

What other furred
and feathered folk
blend with the shadows
I cannot tell;
or if I see small figures
in the pool of moon
beside the shed.

Or if, bewitched,
I am deprived of sense.

# Mirror

I polish wood,
and I can see the wooded farm
and living tree,
slanted fingers of the sun
in clearings,
breath of frost on leathered leaves,
paths that hairpin down the hill
to streams where horses drink,
springhouse water
cool and sweet
pressured up the hill to meet
the needs of farmhouse.

Fingers touch a carpet
made of leaf and log
returned to earth,
and hemlock needles.
It is the fertile womb of moss
and fern and winterberry,
mound of ground pine;
red woods of the lilliputian folk
who live in forests.

I polish wood,
and I can see
a table set with extra places,
unmatched chairs and
phantom faces—oh, the faces!

Fireplace built of native stone
deep and wide
to hold the logs that
hiss and grumble into flame;
pushing back the cold
and shadows.

I polish wood,
and I can see the figures
of both friend and tree.

# Empty Nests and Oak Trees

Oak trees are tenacious.
They hoard their leaves in winter
like women
webbed with wrinkles
wrapped in shawls
hold on to years;
knowing well
that in the long run
all must go
but by their nature
not disposed
to make it easy for the wind
or to accommodate
the reaper.

# Homing

Birds in great formations
swirl like flags across the sky,
then settle down among the trees
to count their congregation.
> They pull out road maps for the flight.
> This way is best for the journey.

The wet-earth smell of maple leaves,
their dancing days now over,
mingles with wood smoke,
blends with smoke-gray sky.
> I hug my arms to keep them warm.
> There is work to be done before winter.

I think I am one month ahead
in evenings with a fire.
Snow swirls, not birds or leaves,
and wood smoke is lost in the swirling.
> What was it the poet said
> about home—and not deserving?

Music spins a warm cocoon
to isolate the worry.
Our glances speak what word we need
above the evening paper.
> Love accepts, just as we are,
> and ends the journey.

# Ms. Muse

What is the likeness
of an hour
when it is gone?

I have ignored the clock
and household chores
and friends,
and now the need for food
brings back reality.

Here there are some scribbled lines
and more
discarded.
The floor is carpeted
with shapeless thoughts
aborted.

And yet for me
and whoever is a kindred soul,
here is the essence of a golden day;
a human being
known and loved;
a little understanding
stored against the day
when hope is thin
and joy is fragile.

I have spent hours
as one spends
money for a prize
and holds it
in his arms.

# For Hal

And he comes home for dinner,
and sometime near the salad
he will say,
"What did you do today?"
And I will say,
"I raked the leaves
and wrote a poem."

And he, the man of logic
who plots the course of energy by day,
will leave his coffee cup suspended
and hold me with his eyes
as though he had not seen before.

And all at once, I know
that poems are not words.

# To My Love, Found Lately

Our love is childhood's panda bear,
fur worn thin where arms have hugged,
comfortable, warm
tangible
presence,
there for the reaching.

Walking in September woods,
fragile fern frond,
velvet moss,
burning bushes,
holy ground
hemlock cushioned.

Fingers of an April rain
freeing all imagined hurts,
gentle, probing,
warmly cleansing,
bringing peace.

String of pearls,
small, perfect luster,
measured capsules of delight,
secret beauty
lying heavy
in the valley of my breast.

Waves expended
on the shore,
lapping, quiet on the sand,
restless asking,
calm assurance,
love is giving.

# Day in the Park

I had forgotten
how a baby, barefoot
walks on grass.
Tentative
he tries on life
for size;
feels each blade and pebble,
curls his toes in pure delight,
toddles, wavers,
saves himself by sitting down;
gurgles when a butterfly
eludes his chubby fist.

And how spring comes
with blue-jeaned lovers
sitting on the grass
oblivious to
workmen spearing trash
and passersby
and violets.
His fingers feel the coolness
in the hollows
where throat and shoulders meet.

I had forgotten how a cloudless sky
can make old fingers
reach and twine;
how gray hair savors
warmth of sun
and lilac trees,
feeling with the mind
along the crevices
of years.

This misplaced day
one month ahead in the middle of May
has summoned spring
before its time.

# Sometimes I Like to Talk to Myself

In each pinch of earth
  there are whole worlds
    and *no* man shall ever see
      the smallest of the small
        or the largest of the large
        of God's creations.

MARTIN BUXBAUM
*from "His Answer"*

# Conversation with a Squirrel

## I

Outside my kitchen window
a deep white blanket
warms the garden
left to sleep just yesterday.
Miniature snow blower,
the squirrel digs deep,
his treasure map within his head.
Only the tip of his tail shows
like a marker flag on a putting green.

Up with something held between his paws,
he sits erect and turns it around.
I ask politely if I may see,
"A nut—a pine cone—or a ball?
I'll bet you don't have anything at all.
I'll bet you're just a bluff."

He flips his tail
and fluffs his fur.
"You don't suppose I'd tell you
if I were!"

## II

Two young squirrels in my back yard
chase each other, stop in their tracks,
playing statues.
They climb a stem, too fragile for their weight,
and hang there, swaying.
"Whee, look at me.
I can do it with one hand!"

They are not so much squirrels
as little boys.
Leaping and tumbling
end over end
they make a whirlwind of my unraked leaves.

They have me spellbound
wondering if perhaps I am the intruder
and they, the owners of this land,
until I almost offer them
my tender tulip greens
as homage.

## III

My neighbors must think I'm mad
to see me robe-and-slipper-clad
chasing squirrels.

Do you think I planted my garden for you?
Succulent greens served with morning dew?

I warn you—if you eat my tulips,
I'll dig up your acorns!

## IV

The tree consigns
a golden cargo
to my hair.
Leaves await
the slightest breeze
to repossess their beachhead.

This labor's more for love
of being ankle deep
in rustle
than for hope of job
accomplished.

I am kinfolk to the squirrel
who digs a shallow saucer
in my lawn
to hide his apple treasure.

On second thought
I'll put it back.
No other lawn I know
raked clean of leaves
can boast an apple
blooming!

# If It Happen Not in Me

Here in time we make holiday because the
eternal birth which God the Father bore and
bears unceasingly in eternity is now born in
time, in human nature. St. Augustine says
this birth is always happening. But if it
happen not in me what does it profit me?
What matters is that it shall happen in me.[4]

MEISTER ECKHART

[4]*Meister Eckhart,* trans. C. de B. Evans, vol. 1 (New York: John
M. Watkins, 1924), p. 3.

# Prayer

There is something in me
of a child
that hopes for snow for Christmas,
not storm or ice
or whistling wind
but soundless snowflakes
drifting down
to wrap the world.

There is something in me
of a prayer;
a yearning for a world
made clean,
reborn to kindness
and to caring.

God, send down your snow
for Christmas.
Wrap every branch and shrub.
Soften the harshness
of my being;
wash me
with the whiteness
of your love.

# Gloria

I walk beneath the pine
and feel the tuft of snow
a squirrel lets go
upon my head.

The sudden whir of crimson wings
stirs up an avalanche.
A jay, as blue as peacock,
soundly scolds
my clumsiness.

I did not know
until I trespassed
that the trees
were trimmed for Christmas—
and I had thought
that they belonged to me.

# How Shall I Come to Christmas?

The heart makes its journey inward.
It peels away the wrappings,
counts the years of living
one by one.

Balsam needles exhale fragrance,
draped in popcorn freshly strung;
red-cheeked apples, aromatic,
rubbed 'til shining.
There is ritual in the kitchen,
made of cinnamon and clove.
Raisins punctuate a cookie;
yeast bread rises.

Rooms hold secrets, ribbon-tied.
Love, in paper ribbon-tied,
waits and grows
and permeates the walls.
Wreaths make halos for the lamplight,
friendly warmth on lilac snow.
Cedar boughs and hemlock
fill the corners.

Once again the house is still.
Candles probe the shadows.
Stars, intensely burning,
share the wonder.

I come to Christmas on my knees.

## Christmas Eve

Dark clouds dip low.
They drag their burden
on the hills.
A feather mattress full of snow
spills out upon the earth.

Silhouette against the sky
a lonely house
and near, a barn.
Lamplight pours
from door and window.

And I, intent on icy road,
relax my fingers
and my fears.
Love reaches out across the years
to warm the world.

# I Remember Julotta

The morning wakens
like a woman
stretching in her bed.
Across the valley
lights appear in windows.
Popcorn bursting into whiteness.

Shoulders hunched against the cold
and half asleep
the neighbors hurry.
Voices calling greetings
merge with voices
calling greetings
merge with sounds
of footsteps crunching
on the snow.

The volume builds
until it seems a host
of voices
singing,
and I, a shepherd
coming from the hills.

NOTE: *One of the beautiful traditions of Christmas, as it was once celebrated in Sweden, was the early-morning Christmas Day service called Julotta. Before the advent of the automobile and the electric light, families rode to the village church in horse-drawn sleighs. Swathed to their chins in fur rugs and wool blankets, they made their way by torchlight, to the accompaniment of sleigh bells. Transplanted to the New World, Julotta became a beloved custom wherever a handful of Swedes put down their roots. The following is a memory of World War II days, when people left their cars at home and traveled on shanks mare.*

# And All at Once . . .

My sisters' gowns
are pale as moths
that beat their wings
against a lamplight.

Their young men, bow-tied
ring the bell;
they hold the coats
and make a bit of small talk,
say good night,
and I am left behind
to read my book
and dream.

If I am very careful
I can fit beneath the tree,
and when I *almost* close my eyes
the candles shimmer.
Their halos touch and grow
until the tree
is all one dancing light.

I lie here
breathing balsam;
no one in my world
but me,
and all at once
I'm grown
and lovely
as the tree.

# A Candle Is for Christmas

If all the symbols Christmas holds
to speak to me of life and love
were lost,
save one,
I'd light a candle.

One candle
straight and tall and fair
would tell me all my heart could bear.

My fingers on its slender shape
would trace the loveliness
of Mary; its warmth
would speak of oxen near,
their ears pricked up to hear a mother's moan,
a Baby's cry;
their munching sounds, a lullabye.

If all the dear things Christmas holds
to speak to me of love and hope
were lost,
save one,
I'd light a candle.

I'd watch the wax
drip down its side.
A candle gives itself for light.
So . . . God's gift
that trembling night
was born of love and freely given.

# Index of Titles